I0143319

UPLIFTING POETRY

for self-love, hope, and healing

Leia Leh

PEACOCK FEATHER PRESS
An Imprint of L.L. Sage Studio
Suffern, New York
LLSage.com

Uplifting Poetry for Self Love, Hope and Healing

Copyright © 2025 by Leia Leh
All rights reserved.

No part of this book may be reproduced, stored in a retrieval system, or transmitted in any form or by any means — electronic, mechanical, photocopying, recording, or otherwise — without prior written permission of the publisher, except for brief passages in connection with a review.

ISBN 979-8-9985225-2-9 (hardcover)
ISBN 979-8-9985225-0-5 (paperback)
ISBN 979-8-9985225-1-2 (ebook)
First Edition: September 2025

To

_____

From

_____

For Shani

your radiance transcends miles

It all began with a gift...

A while back, a dear friend gave me a beautiful journal—too special for everyday thoughts. I set it aside, waiting for inspiration. One day it hit me: it would be the perfect place to jot down my poems. From then on, I kept it beside my Julia Cameron–style morning-pages journal, ready whenever a poem began to brew. And that's how this collection of poetic letters was born.

Life pulled my friend and me in different directions, the way life does when it gets busy. And as I filled the pages, I found myself writing in a way that felt comforting, like having her nearby, even if we weren't talking every day. No plan to ever share them—just a quiet way to stay connected in my own little way. Some pieces are light, some helped me make sense of things, and some feel like quiet little convos with angels above.

Before I knew it, this became my morning flow—poems and morning pages, with coffee, of course. And just like that, I reached the last page. Nearly a year had passed since I first opened that journal, and the timing was surreal. My friend's birthday was coming up—the same friend who had gifted me the journal in the first place. I knew immediately what I wanted to give her.

I typed my poems, had them printed into a book, and sent them her way. We were on the phone together as she opened the package. Her reaction moved me to tears. And that's when I realized—it was the strongest of whispers: this book was meant to be shared.

I felt it in my soul—these poems, these "letters in friendship," carry a loving-kindness that's meant to be passed on.

Now this book is in your hands, which means it's meant for you, too. My hope is that it keeps traveling, from one friend to another —a gift to share, especially when life makes being together a little more challenging. Just a gentle reminder that true friendship doesn't need to live in the same city or country to be deeply nourished.

The poems are in the exact order they were written, unfolding over nearly a year. If you read them that way, maybe you'll feel the seasons shift, the emotions change, the way life keeps moving.

And if you ever find yourself feeling somewhat alone, I hope these words remind you that you're not. You are held, you are seen, and you are so loved. And as you turn these pages, I hope they bring you back to believing, dreaming, and living a life that feels uplifted.

"We delight in the beauty of the butterfly, but rarely admit the changes it has gone through to achieve that beauty."

— Maya Angelou

Your words touch my heart
Your warmth, your care
It's as if we were sisters
in another life, and so we are

What would you tell me now
if I were to open up this box—
not Pandora's, mine

I wish to lighten its load
or perhaps, its content to fold
into a manageable size
that is easy on the eyes

Instead, I continue to stuff
it all in. Much as I thought
I changed. In some ways
I wonder

Living uplifted, in spite of
or because of.

This morning, early, but not that
two hummingbirds swam before me
Is that even a word? Swam, swum

No matter. Fly they did not.
Acrobats are more of their kind
You know, the ones in water

Dancing. It brings to mind
thoughts flitting through the air
then diving deep, burying despair

This is how I find myself
on this day's break, mist felt—
feels as a spring cleaning

Showering me
with fresh delights
simple sights, though magical

I send them on, to you my dear
Energy of their wings
songs they sing, only we hear.

Things are not always what they seem
Underneath the mundane are waves of joy
waiting to be released. And yet, I stand
holding back, not sure why, afraid to cry

For if I did, the rivers would spill
into oceans, onto lands, and what then—
Where would I stand, where would you?
Where would we be, us two?

Upon rafts, floating, on sailboats, singing
With sun shining—taking us, showing us
to islands remote, filled with abundance
fruit aplenty, of all our labor transformed

So perhaps it's time
I let go of the grime
Shed a tear for the past. Join me at last
Let's set sail, without fail, to better days

Awaiting.

***Lately, a thread making its way**
Purpose, woven tight
between lines, so bright
Giving strength—forming its whole
from three; one pulled together
a second, just now
the third, twisted somehow
around both—lifeline for the ages*

*What source is its flexibility?
Perhaps of futuristic technology—
Not! Rather of decades past
centuries, eons, peering forward*

*There she is dancing free
interloping with you and me
Presence to witness, not to tame
Flickering around us, as a flame*

*Love
a mother's, unhindered
sets the rules, so it is
Permission to unravel—
weave your dreams tight
Unbreakable, unstoppable
such strength, who knew?!
But of course, my darling
               she too, is You.*

What if you mothered yourself
as you mother your child
What if I did?
Would anything change?

My message to me, would be:
Sweetheart, why must you work
so hard, try so hard, look so hard
Breathe, my darling, enjoy the day
Relax my darling, all will be ok
You've gone through enough
When will it be—enough?!

Motek, metuka, child of mine
We've all suffered in the past
Now is the time
Open your eyes, see the cake—
made it for you, a piece do take
Have a second, it's yours
Indulge in sweetness, in sweet

I want you to be happy, so be
Bake a life of ease
Add honey, my honey
                    please.

What if I told you I felt lost
among thoughts that do not serve?

You'd rescue me, sword and shield
slashing each, laying them to rest
in a field afar. I know you can
yet I am capable, too
of seeing the truth, that lies—
the lies that hide underground

What if though, I took each one
cradled it, instead? Asked you
to bring sunflower and seeds
Fill my mind, my soul with ease
with dreams and goals to ignite—
delight! Ah, I should have known
that is your super flower
Those are your powers—ours.

Amazing, isn't it, how with time
we catch up with ourselves—
catch ourselves in a place sublime
What happens though, to the days
in between—a haze, a daze

Why did I let a year pass
before doing the thing? The nurturing
of my soul. Neglecting the call
while, all the while, while waiting...
For what? Today. Yesterday
When all along I was free to grab it

No matter now, I did
Regrets now, I rid.

Feeling a stir in the air
Leaves swirling, lifting
Colors of autumn in purples and pinks
Unlike anything we've ever seen.

Dreams, wishes, wants and hopes
Grasping at this one and that
The ones I manage to keep and hold
I press, flattening them between pages
My way of preserving through the ages

One day you will open this book
See the remnants of that hope I took
Run your finger over its veins
Understanding that life still remains

Forever yours.

How often are we rescued from harm
Saved without hearing the alarm
Yesterday was such a day
Only this time, calm I did stay

Noticing, aware of my self
Wondering how this was different
Not the situation, bizarre as it was
But me, at peace, believing

On wings of an eagle, untouchable
Connected, knowing, soaring
Doing what I must
Trust.

Looking up at the great tree
What I see, shelters me
Canopy, the leaves of angels
Above my roof, dancing, swaying
As if proof
Choices I made, here and in heaven

Going the right way, I count to seven
Simply because it rhymes

I like to play that way
Climbing up the branches
Starting a new day
New life, no longer on a limb
Feeling steady, held up, protected
From above and within.

Wondering how you are
Both of us seem afar
From dreams, wishes, desires
Busy putting out the fires

Yet we are closer than we know
All we need to do is go
To that place beneath our lids
Darkness, where we hid
The best part of our being
Connecting with it is seeing
That all we want is here

Open your eyes to mine, my dear
Welcome to your sweet new year.

Trees, for miles it seems, high
If I climbed, should I dare?
Would anyone miss me—
Would anyone care?

I know they would
Why do I bother to ask—
It's just one of those moments
Wondering—the point of task
That lies before me
Of living a life, different
Marching to the beat of my brush
Stroke by stroke, without the rush
No need to succeed
At anything
Other than doing what I was
Put here to do—my thing
Figuring out what it is, a puzzle
I thought—in actuality, it's easy
Stepping aside so that I can thrive
Allowing for my destiny to come alive
Maybe, living this way for a year...

Suddenly, it all becomes quite clear
The point, the reason, the way
That I matter, and when
Is simply in being one with this pen.

What do you do when you reach
Point of destiny, dreamed
When a hope and a prayer
Arrives, at last

Me, on such a day, I dance
I am now, within
As I was before, without
Free of the burden, I move

Or was it because I did?

No matter, no need, I breathe
With you, I share, I believe.

Words falling from the sky
My pen is an open net
Forming, over the years
Decades passed, holes patched
Finally able to gather
The ones that matter
Bringing them to you
Bouquet of the undescribed
Blooms as the ink of my stem
Grows petals, nurtured by your sunshine.

I'm at a crossroads
unfamiliar
Yet intention lies within
Forming the path ahead of me
Not quite clear, but there

It's only a matter of time
Before it becomes the past
Interesting, isn't it—
If it was revealed
at this very moment, would I take it?
Most likely yes, because I made it
Dreamed it
Or did I? This destiny is mine
So gone is the worry, the hurry
I will reach it, I am enjoying it, I am

The I here is Divine
The I here is not mine
Me, but a bystander
Fortunate to witness
Life unfolding
Delivering to me
All that is meant to be
To see, to feel, to heal
Embracing it—this time
This round, me's attached to I
Unseparated, liberated
At last.

Alone, at last

Thought it's what I wanted
Knowing it's what was needed
To contemplate what was lost
All that was nurtured and left
To unfold its wings, to fly
Another sky, beckoning me
Don't you see? It's not as simple
As they made it look, those angels
Sages of the book

Perhaps that's part of the struggle
Yet if it is, the juggle
I rest my balls. Gone is the bounce
What's left is air within
Contained, accepting what remains
It's time to play a new game
Rollin' with it, on my own, together.

That sounded depressing
It was not meant to be so
Simply stating the rhythm
Beat of a drum in-between
Stanzas awaiting, building
Up to a crescendo
I'm there, in mind and soul
At the tip of all I know
Awaits sun, cities, worlds
Celebrating life without strife
If you notice me looking down
Trust not that impression
Fleeting it is.

__Isn't it awe-inspiring, watching__
Waiting for a new day
Witnessing without doing
Though I have, many times over
This time I get to simply be
Receive the gift
Connect, care
Hoping to, this year
In a way that is light
Awaiting all that is bright.

At the tip of an iceberg
Cold, frozen, I'm not
Warming me are dreams
Calling to what I've got
Do you feel it, sense it?
Change in the air
Ice melting, cracking
Make way, love appears
Reflections on the lake
Break, for a New Year.

Settling into a new sense of peace
This one feels different, unknown
To me, how this can be
With all that transpired

Or perhaps because of it—

Yes, that's it, a privilege
For the few who have traveled
Heavy sacks on their back
For miles, through a desert of tears

Cracked earth, a dandelion
Somehow made it through
You're looking at this weed of
Sunshine, a miracle—that she grew

Yet here I am with you.

How does one celebrate
Life so dear? Precious
When we but witnessed
Its arrival, miracles
Many surround us, walking
Talking up a storm
Dreaming of an oasis
Where we sing and dance
As if in a trance
Marveling this new beginning
Cheering the awe, this feeling
How fortunate we are
To be living.

They tell me there's not enough
I say there's plenty

They tell me, Be real!
I say, Do you see what I feel?

Mountains I carry
Oceans I drink
Birds I lift
With my pinky

Keep dreaming the sky
I tell them, I may—I do

Sharing my world with you.

Stillness

Birds from another time and place
Listening to them transports me
Back, then forward, when all I want
Is to stay here for a minute
Even as I write the moment passed
What can I do to make it last?
Perhaps that is what calls me forth
The will to pen my very north
Why do I resist it so?
When the ink flows like water
Holding on to lead, I did
Traded pencils for paint
For that reason
Letting go of all that was
Picturing a new season

Still, the birds chirp.

Butterfly upon my wall
Listening quietly to it all
Taking it in as an observer
Wanting more for me
For you, too, it can be!

Transformation occurred.

How? When?
Overnight it seems
Yet, what a stretch of darkness
It was... and now— flutters
Excitement buds, hope blossoms

She's off, wings spread wide.

In a new place, ethereal is it
The word to describe this feeling
Sitting in it, susspended—
The extra S for secrets, worries
Letting go of all that, hovering
Above, with love, seeing it now
The bigger picture, the reason for
All that was, is the now
Me with you, writing here with—
Sister dear, do you feel it?
The silence has a sound, Serenity
Yes, traded it in, that which
Was, for the peace that is—
                Shhh, it's between us.

How is it that a mood can bounce

Dancing one minute
        bungee jumping
                the
                    next

Catching myself midair
        righting this spirit dear

Too much is at stake
        won't leave it to the winds of
                        Chance.

Between us, pure white sands
I've traveled them
     skipped through lands
Immersed in waters
     purified my soul
Now at peace
     so why a new goal?
Can't that be enough—
     to sit and be free?
Yet I hear this call, pulling me
     pulling me
        to another oasis.

Presumptuous of me, perhaps
To say I know what you're thinking
Feeling, as I was
Oblivion would sometimes be
State preferred—no!
Life is sweet, oh, so sweet
Pull yourself into this minute
Paper smooth, the color divine
Penned thoughts can be
Sublime
Ignoring? I am not—
But at times like these
It's all I've got.

Feeling grateful.

Is it wrong to feel right
When the world is in fright
Is it shameful to feel hopeful
When the news is so awful?
This too shall pass
Is what I hear, Angels
Whispering in my ear
While we cry, they sigh
And pray for us
Wish for us. Dance for us
to live—joyfully

Our light
shall
stay lit
See to it! So be it.

It will be okay
Up there
> *It already is*
>> *What do we know?*
What do we truly understand?
> *Other than it's our job*
> *Our place, our service*
> *To lift, to love, to light*
> *To serve our Creator*
> *With trust and kindness*
> *And yes—with joy*
Perhaps that is why it is
> *A commandment—*
> *It isn't always so simple*
> *But it can be*
>> *With simplicity*
>> *Believe, pray*
>> *Trust, pray*
> *Trust*
>> *Believe, pray*
Do good, Be
> *Live good, pray*
>> *To Life.*

I'm not fully sure why
My words fall as a preacher's
Are they even mine?
Did I hear them from—
source, Divine?
They must be, because
Here I am, but a child
Listening, learning, hoping
That I live up to
my purpose, as you are.

How can I explain
That which is above
Sane
I am, disconnecting
Fully, happily, I must
Trust
This is the way to be
Clarity, finally.

Service—with joy

How to connect
But to reflect
On that which is
Giving way
Water rushing
Gushing, Giving
Yes, I use that—
The word—twice
Thrice now, Giving
You, the gift of my love
　　　　　From Above.

Embarking on a new path

Yet remnants remain

Using them as gravel

To shield heavy rain

Seeds below

Beginning to grow

Me hesitant, holding onto

What? Dreams, wishes

I sprinkle them upon

What is

Watching now, waiting now

For magnificence to perform

Majestic acts—Blossoming

Watch, witness

Here they come.

Don't you worry about me
I'm held up from Above
Invisible string
It's my thing
To swing from limb to limb
Catching drift of whispers and whim
Being propelled, pulled, lifted
Where, I cannot yet say
Trust me though, when I tell you this
G♡D is showing me the way.

What if I don't want to
Talk today
What if I just want to
Sit in play
Would that be okay?
Why do I feel the need
To ask this, indeed!
What if I just let go
Let myself fall into flow
What would I be doing then—
I'd write you The Story, a dance with my pen.

I am okay

New chapter, that's all
A bit of unknown, that's all
Stepping out of my comfort, that's all
Got to take better care of myself, that's all
While trusting all is coming from Above, with love

Intentions becoming
Creating a life of lift and lilt
Yes, what happened to that?
Intend to
Recapture the thought
Make it real, I am

While trusting
All is coming from Above, with love.

Excitement is in the air
Can you feel it?
I am holding you dear
Can you see it—
Sparkles surround us
Beneath our soles, too
Lifting us, tickling us
Infusing joy, delight, love
In all we do, in all we are
Essence of stars.

Here, too, silence reigns strong
Words underneath
wish to burst into song
Yet, a barrier, a frost
breaks through from within
Won't happen that way
let the rain soak in
Yup, it's got to come from above
Did all that we can
To nurture our dreams
building homes in the sand
By the water, if only—
no, ours are here
Been open to relocate
jump ahead through the years
Our time is coming
palace on solid ground
In this courtyard, in the rain
we dance without a sound.

Hope is on the horizon
Looking brighter than ever before
Colors of sunset sprinkled
On this lake of life, me at the shore
Squinting so I can take in
The marvel that unfolds before me
Glimmers are but raindrops
On my tongue, mouth open
To the blessings of stories
Filling my days, my time here on earth
Enriched by your presence
Embracing my worth
My roots reaching for the sun
All the past, undone
Here I stand humble and bare
Gone is the shadow, gone is the fear
All of me is sun and sea
Moving toward eternity
While in this moment taking in
The beauty of here
       As the world slowly spins
Grasping tight, loosening my grip
Now a gentle hold, Heaven above, within.

Feeling your vibes
Shaking
Sending you mine
Solid
Is it? Touched by yours
Swaying
Arm in arm
Oceans apart
Heart to heart
Connected
Comforted by waves—
Today's serene sea
Tenderly loving you, loving me.

Moving so fast, the days
Even more—
Time, wanting to catch up
With my dreams
Velocity, intense
Reaching for the walls
Feeling air, wind
Spinning me forward
Wanting to go—
Yet resisting the flow
Why do I?
Holding onto old habits
Is what I know, knew
Discarding them now
With this flow of ink
Lest I sink—I shall not!
From this day, I welcome
Breeze and ease
With open arms
Now swirling in song
Twirling
The frenzy has slowed
To a dance.

What can I say?
A week flew by in the blink of an eye
While I transformed under a starless sky
Blanketed being, unaware of the changes
Pressed to conform no more
Yet, imposing a blindfold
Which I now remove, squinting
At all that's in store
Has me wanting to pull the covers back up
I grasp for the comfort of naiveté
Only to feel the calm, cool air
Of possibilities. Now, a gentle rain
Taps my brow. I look up. I'm looking up.

And how are you?
Do you feel the morning dew, too?

Why do wings hurt before they grow?
Why the time to learn and sow?

All that I've planted, kind of left aside
Been praying for sun—but then I hide

Did my hands help in clearing the weeds?
Or did I nurture the wrong kind of seed?

I wonder now at what felt so right—
Were they Silver Dollars dangling in sight?

Maybe it's best to put shades on and hope
Pray for a miracle of grand epic scope

But no, that's not what I came here to do
Putting my gloves on and gardening anew.

And just like that

My year is transformed
Clarity, Focus, Direction
Gifted to me
Clearest of seas
  Not looking down
    But up from below
To the sun shining
Reflecting glimmers
      Waves
        I rise
And just like that
        I praise.

It happened again
I let it somehow
Slip of a thought
Justification of naught
No biggie, I said
Now I'm in bed
When will I learn
To do as I yearn
Protect the energies
Of flow
Today I declare
To hold myself dear
    letting go of yesteryear.

Getting up

Slowly I rise
From a stupor, misplaced
       hocus-pocus, focus!

Feels as if someone
             waved a wand
Above my head, shouted:
       Live as you instead!

So today marks the day
I stick to my intention
Not mine really, correction—

Path set from Above
       Upon wings of a dove
          Reward is my joy
             Becoming.

Starting fresh
    with a cup of juice
Squeezed sweet
       by all that was
Filled my glass
          filling
            learning
Am I?
    I believe I just did.

It's been a while
Us going—where?
Winds of change
Bringing us back
To who we are
No need to swim upstream
One job we have—is dream!
Of the day we sit
Me and you
Candles lit
Story or two
    of the years
        that were—
Leading us
    to this very moment.
        Swing on!

How does one put into words
Feelings from another world
How does one begin to hold
Emotions of a thousandfold
What I experienced yesterday
Was a bliss of proportions unmet
That is, until the day was spent
With me in awe from what it took
To detach from every pull and hook
There I was, fish in the sea
Swimming, breathing in my eternity
Connecting, sharing, eye to soul
With guests at my table—whole
Yes, that is it—the word, the feel
Complete and on purpose, I begin to heal.

How've you been?
Me—where am I?
You ask and I'll tell
But please keep it still
Quiet, hush, secret wish
To float up in the air
man a spaceship
It's not what you think—
I'm loving this thing called life
For once though, I dream
Of different
Holding onto my peace
my loves so dear
Only transport me
To where the air is clear.

What's that about?

Concern yourself not
Just having a moment
That's all
Needed to unload the weight
I put on at the gate
Walking through it
Dumping the old—
The torn, damaged and broken
Leaving all the unspoken
Running towards sunshine
Smiling now
Spring showers awakening
It will be awesome

                          Is now.

Thanks

For walking me through
Feeling lighter, brighter
Gone is the blue
Purple is back, yup, that's me
Regal, royal, playful as can be
Trusting as always
That my castle is awaiting
I only read books with happy
      Endings—are beginnings
         Aren't they?

What a difference
A day can make
Can bring
   Make your heart sing
Mine does now
      Gone is the frown
Almost forgot this feeling
Bubbles rising
         Sense of glee
Feeling time by my side
      Dancing with me.

Worlds are splitting
Forming two where one was
Was it ever?
Each in their own orbit, spun
Meeting together, melding
Occasionally
To create worlds better
Than they ever were
Or perhaps they are
Now, soon
Becoming stars
As they were meant, designed
To Be.

There are remnants
Of the old life
Pulling, calling me back
Resisting the urge
Grabbing, grasping
At rocks, crevices
Where I can plant
My palms and hold on
Holding on, I am
Climbing out of that pit
The valley, I leave
Sunshine is close
I'm almost there
Saying goodbye
Moving up
With all I hold dear
Held in the pockets
Of my heart
Lightweight
Yet strong
Propelling me
To my future

Stopping here
To catch my breath
Looking back, only to see
An ocean calm, deep Serenity.

Daffodils await
  Children's laughter
        Birds chirping
      Books with worlds
       Filled with smiles

Almost there
  Hold on my dear
      Keep stretching
            To the sun

Before you know it
     The day will come
          Stay uplifted.

What is here
Canvas complete
For now
Intentionally declaring
It is
Can I add more, sure
Should, could, would
Plays on
Resisting the urge
Takes courage
Today I stand
For being
Enough

And so I am.

Energy, stuck
  Not stagnant
    Excited, alive
      Yet
        Flow has paused
Why on this day
    At this moment
        Do I falter?

You were not born to be a horse
Pause for breath—it's part of the course
    Falter? You are not
        Merely a need to refill your cup
        Let the moment pass
It surely will
In the meantime fill, darling, fill.

Evening, stars
Out and about
I'm dancing, jumping
From one to the other
All the while
Holding myself back
From the one shining
Brightest, beckoning
Why, oh why
Am I afraid? Not at all
It's but a hesitance—of leaping too soon
Don't want to insult the moon

They think they own each other
Each a diamond in the sky
If only they knew, as do I
Their beam, sparkle, ray and lens
Is but a mere reflection, a connection
Separate them and the sun still smiles
True radiance transcends miles
When that happens—it will, it will
Then I will hop, skip and jump, until
Me and the stars are one
      Waltzing till morning's dawn.

Morning has its way
> Bringing merriment
> When clouds drift away

I tell them
> When they show up

Uninvited
> Opening my arms

In warm welcome
> To memories of smiles

Possibilities wild
> Good morning, my sweet
>> It is.

Water on each side

Doing my best to walk
While the little one
Wants to run
To flee, be free
As young ones do
You know it's true
Things of the past
Somehow have a way
A want
To catch up, capture...

Drown it all!
Noise that chatters
Keeps us from what matters
Praying, praying
Keeps me on this path
To your warmth
Sunshine and love
Paper blossoms
Homes in vibrant color
Upon lands await
I keep up, speed up my gait
Hand in hand, hearts as one
Crossing to the other side
Me, smiling wide
There's no turning back now.

What if we were
Next-door neighbors
My coffee would runneth over
With the taste of sharings
Carings, laughter and love
Tea in between
Pairings from Above
Not much would get done
No, not an ounce
Better we move worlds
From afar
Connected by the same star.

Hey, are you okay?
Your words are strained
I read between the lines—

You haven't given time for you
To play, imagine something new

How dare I assume, when
Your effort leaves no room
For anything other than praise

It's the child in you
Calling me when you're busy
Asking to make time
*   to spin a dime*
*   or a rhyme*
*   Will you?*

I'm not far behind
My little one inside
Beckons too, for new
Letting go
Unstuck from the muck
Showered, fresh
White as a dove
Filled with what-if
Imagining in color
Life's about to start
Soaring in wonder.

Hesitance, to start the day
Ripping that feeling to shreds
Excited now for what's ahead
Butterflies dancing above my bed

Bringing wishes to life
Thoughts connected
Angels stirring, sifting
Baking a cake—joy's at stake

I take a slice, share it with you
Cheers to our dreams coming true.

Letting go today

Past misconceptions
Attached as I've been
Thought it was the answer
Apparently not
Amazing, isn't it
How we tend to hold on
As if it's all we've got
Perhaps it was, then.

The day calls me
>Do, Do, Go

Sounds like a song
>of toddlers

Feeling as one
  confidently unsteady

 Taking new steps
>turning back

Again
>a bit further forward

Determined to the core
  watch me from the shore—
I'll be running in no time!

This little girl is a champion.

Isn't it lovely
When a flower grows
Unexpectedly
When water flows
Upon dry land
When a song is sung
In quiet stand
Yesterday was such a day
I wake and wonder
What sweet kindness
Is next on the horizon

I wonder, too—what did I do
To deserve it being this way
Perhaps it's not
Because of what I did
But because of who I am:
Soul
Sunshine, sea, fruit and tree
Bird, a feather, flying free

Oh, what a world G♡D made
          for you and me.

Flexibility is key
At least it seems
Been pushing instead
Of letting go
Why the obsession
Fixation on design
Of the past
Which served its purpose
Set it aside
Ready for a new ride
What wasn't meant to be
Will transform into beauty
                    in time.

Getting off the plane
Liberated
Why then
Is discipline needed
Now, more than ever
Starting a new life
Free of strife
Takes courage
Have heart, will travel

To the star where you are
I'm so close
Wait for me, sister dear
I'll be there soon—
Please set our table on the moon.

Another birthday
    Must take stock
Of the changes
    In me, with glee
Why then, a sense of
    Heavy—
Forgot to unload
The bag of coals
Burnt memories cooked up a sweet life
Wouldn't trade them in now—
               No, not ever!
Still, perhaps I can scatter them
    At the base
Of the great oak tree
    Woman of Wonder
    Archaic and free
She won't mind
    In fact, you'll find
Acorns will dance beside them
Old and new, rocks and dew
Have a way of breathing together
Leave them be
    Soon you'll see
Figments of imagination
      Swirling
          Unearthing
              Treasures.

Sleep calls

Why won't I respond?
Holding on to a shell
Glimmer of a day done
If I succumb
What will become
Of this moment
Already it passed
Wasn't meant to last
All that remains is this note.

(Ah, then, perhaps this is—
Alchemy at its finest.)

Today marks the first of May

Not an actuality

In productivity

In possibility

I may transform

Once again

You may not recognize

All the change

Then again you might

My wings are still purple.

The hour is not the one
I aimed for
Let it go
With the clouds
Catching hold of fresh ones
Those are mine
All is as it should be
Time can be
Sublime

Let it be.

Three marks a charm
Or is it three times
No matter
Had one more to give you
The one I intended
At the start
My heart
Can barely contain the excitement
Did you see the eclipse?
All is clear now—clearer than ever
I begin.

The sun and moon met
Same for my loves
Closer, closer
They merge
As one—one day

I am weaving
At the loom, I am
Soon I will teach others
The way that is:
To unravel
Is the way to create a new
Everlasting love.

It's not easy to part
Sitting with you
Is my heart
Yet the day calls me
Away
A way
To get closer to you
In all that I do
I remain
To us

Devoted.

Just one more

>> *to say*

>>> *it's been a while*

I do hope you're okay

That your dreams are lived

>> *with joy and ease*

That your tears dried with spring

>> *now in the air*

>>> *sun in your hair*

Would you please post me a note—

>>> *in song?*

Sending you sweet chords of care.

Consider this part of the past
Doing my best to make good last
Perhaps that's where I went wrong
Been spinning the same old song

Okay, then here's another:

Soaring on wings of my pen
Brushes of paint playing again
Coloring our world vivacious
Soul sister, aren't we courageous?!

Yesterday I did the not easy
Today I'm feeling sore, but breezy
I know if I repeat the steps
My body will adjust

Flowing with the rest
My mind
Liberated
From all that held me back

Perhaps these sensations remain
Only to keep me on track
Is it the same for you?
Permission to feel and let it go, too.

Soul poetess
Has charm, wouldn't you say?
Describing us on a better day
When we distance
Ourselves
From the fluff
The mundane
Singing words on paper
Others wonder is she sane
Dreamland where we live
You and I both
Believing in good
In kindness
In love
In a world of peace
How dare we
Be in our bubble
Shield ourselves from trouble—
If only they knew
What it takes
To hold up the pain
Pamper it, pacify it
Transform it into hope
Send it up to the heavens
To play with the stars
Singing us to sleep
As we try not to weep—

instead, we smile
We dance
We force ourselves
Into a trance
Until that becomes
Sunshine for the weary
Disposing of the dreary
Strength for the ones
Who held on too long
Yes, right every wrong
Is what we dream of
In song
In our own little way
By not succumbing to fear
Instead, choosing to steer
Towards kindness, peace and love
With guidance from Above.
This ain't no easy ride—
Blessed, I am, to have you by my side.

Why is it that a reset
Is needed
Most mornings?
When will my default
Be, one of
Absolute certainty
What if today
I say
Expect good things!
Yes, I shall
Time for a new song—
Bird's at my window
Sending a note on to you
This one's uplifting
Soon you'll hear it, too.

Don't you wish you could press Presto
Have every idea, want and wish
Done and set upon your favorite dish
Walter, oh, waiter—Angel of mine!
Been waiting on my order
                    Isn't it time?

Another day
>   *Expecting good things*
What joys will it
>   *Bring*
Sunshine
>   *And sweetness*
I must start baking
>   *So it may rise*
Soon—
For you, a tasty surprise.

Sinking my toes in warm sand
Cares slipping away
Bubble bath
Undersea
Cave of pure serenity
Others wonder
Where I am
When not doing all I can
Find me—don't
Please let me be
For a simple moment
Eternity.

Sometimes I tend to
    My garden of thoughts
            Overthinking
            Overworking
Pulling up weeds
      And a flower!
Didn't mean to
      Oh, the power!
Placing it in a glass
      Please, make it last

Slowing down
      Gone is my frown

Petals calling me to play
      Letting go of cares today.

Wondering what I meant
    Words and images
        I sent
Out into the world
        too early
Better then, than not
        at all
Your dress is sweet
    My belle of the ball.

How dear it is
     to sit with you
         and stew
Takes time to make
       a meal
         to heal
All that was
      and more

Sip, sip, this soup
   it's good for you
Sip, sip, for me, too
Nothing quite compares, erases made-up fears

Suddenly all is looking up—lifting my cup
Blinking the tears away
Today's a fresh new day
Dessert is coming for us to share
        Hurry, darling, spoons prepare!

Today I took the road
  less taken
At least by those
  who walk
Discovered a book
  when I took a look

Worlds collide in stride

Skipping now with
  my new acquisition
About to give birth to my latest edition:
    Me.

Skies are clearer today
Can see the distance
Between me and the tree
The one
Over the ocean
Propped up on dreams

Took my oars, pedaling fast
Got me nowhere—faster
Trick is to bring them close
Each one resting near
Current is, as current does
Pulling me toward my loves

Realizing now, slowing pace
Helps me to win this race
Against my mind
        Heart champions all

Soaring now—
        You ask me how
Remember my oars?
        They're wings now
Meet you on the moon
        My darling dear
Flap your feathers
    We've got much to share!

Words seem to hover
 Between worlds
  On this morning
   I find myself
Peering through a lens
 Clear as the waters
  I wade in
Crystals above
 Cradled in love
No one needs understand
 The ways of our land
  As long as—
   We have each other.

Grateful for the one
  who raised his voice not
Gentle as the breeze
        on a summer day
We may not agree
        nor see eye to eye
Yet his caring, by me
        is the epitome
        of effort
In bridging the gap
Of the forest that grew between us

Tree by tree I make my way
  Swinging, climbing, crawling on days
Again upright
  Running with all my might
        Toward belief—praying for relief

So close we are, can't you tell?
        Angels surround us—hush, listen:
        "All will be well."

My heart swells for this gentle soul
    Especially so
      Invested I am
        Since we are
Connected before birth
    Aware of his worth
Defending it, with my all—
              I shall, I am!
This diamond in my care
    Brilliance will appear
Devoted, day in and out
    Polishing, sweating, doing the work
Soon is the time—to sit back with wine
Watch him shine, Radiant
        Divine
        Sweet child of mine.

Have you felt me with you
Each morning?
Connected by merely a thread
Yet one so strong
It can hold up a world—
Bead strung in its center

Ours spinning
Clock ticking
Hands meeting
Hearts beating as one

Distance is but an illusion
Time may cause confusion
Yet I know the truth we seek
Peace is not for the meek
Glad I have a warrior in you
The prize—sweet serenity for two.

Been putting off
This letter
Its weight—not a feather
By any means
What I must share
Sit down my dear
I am leaving
Going afar
Not sure if I'll be back
'I' won't—not as 'I' am
Despair not!
My love you've got
The road ahead is golden
May take a day, a month
A year, no matter
I'll bring you treasures
(not trinkets—gold!)
Have faith in time
Goodness unfolds
Let not sway your
Hope for better
Better it will be
For you and for me
Blessings for all—eternity.

Writing you is writing me
Loving you is loving me
Connected we are
Dreaming afar

Becoming who we are
Born to be—
Sweet, sensational
Sparkles of light, delight!

Thank you for skipping
Along with me
On this wondrous journey
Though magic not, it's magical

Words cannot describe
Feelings I hide

Sharing them with you
As we hold hands
Tears melt into laughter
Playing in the sand

Building castles among stars
Because we can—because we are
Guided from Above
With unconditional Love.

Darling,
     keep singing your song
For a lifetime long—
     a hundred years
          plus twenty more
I'll be dancing with you at the shore.

An end is the mark of a new beginning.

About the Author

Leia Leh (lay-ah leh) is the founder of LL Sage Studio and a soulful creator of books, art, and Soul Notes self-love cards. Her middle name, Leiba—meaning "love" in Hebrew, reflects the heart of her work. From her home in Rockland, NY, she pours her care into works that inspire hope, healing, and a deeper connection to life. Whether through words, art, or shared experiences, her creations uplift, empower, and invite readers to rediscover their own spiritual essence.

Get insider studio updates from Leia at **LLsage.com/studio**

Acknowledgements

With heartfelt gratitude to G♡D—for life, love, family, friendship, and the creative spirit that flows through me.

Among the invaluable friendships woven into this collection's journey, I begin by celebrating Sara Shani Zimmerli.

Thank you for the beautiful sage-colored suede journal in which these poems were first born—and for gifting me your presence as they poured onto the pages. You were always in my heart and mind as I wrote. We met during coach training at the Co-Active Institute, and our soul-sister bond has enriched my life ever since. I could fill a book with all the sweet sentiments I want to express to you… but I suppose in writing this book, I already have. Thanks for inspiring its creation and traveling beside me on life's wondrous ride.

A huge hug of thanks to my sister, Sarah Weiss, for her gracious hospitality in sunny Florida. There, I found three uninterrupted days of bliss—humming along while typing up all my handwritten poems. Sweetest Sarah'le—know that I am forever grateful.

To my treasured, talented friends Cindy Yang and Dontia Vereen- Thank you for dancing the creative path with me. We were "randomly" paired in a design course study-buddy group back in 2022—though I don't believe anything is truly random. It felt divinely orchestrated. We've been meeting online almost weekly ever since, and it was magical to meet in person at the MOMA in New York City. Your encouragement and steady support have been both precious and priceless to me. Cindy, thank you too, for the brilliant idea to bring my butterfly doodles to life—flipbook style. They add a delightful touch of wonder to these pages.

I also extend my heartfelt thanks to the eight fabulous friends who generously volunteered as early readers of this book:

Cindy, Dontia, Paula, Sheri, Sachiko, Shani, Susan, and Ilene— Thank you for opening your hearts to these poems. Your reflections on how the words moved, comforted, and resonated with you brought me to tears. Your feedback validated what I felt deep down that this book is meant to be shared.

A very special thank you to Susan Cain and her *The Quiet Life* Substack community, of which I'm grateful to be a member. When I shared my poem *"What if you mothered yourself…"* in the comments, the kind responses filled me with warmth and gratitude. I love how words from the soul can reach another without us ever needing to meet. It feels right to honor that connection by placing this particular poem (a personal favorite!) on the back cover.

In Hebrew, there's a saying: *Acharon, acharon, chaviv*—"the last one mentioned is dear."

And so, to you, my dear reader—yes, you. Thank you for picking up this book and spending your time and heart with these pages. I hope something here offers you a moment of serenity, solace, or sparkle. I imagine this book making its way between friends—bridging distances, offering comfort, and showing up at just the right moment. May you feel the hugs tucked between the lines, and I hope you enjoy sharing this book with someone you care about as much as I loved sharing it with you.

Live uplifted,
Leia Leh

A Small Sweet Favor

If you found this book uplifting or simply enjoyable to read, it would truly mean a lot if you could take a quick minute to leave a review about it on Amazon.

Your thoughtful words can **help others discover the love, hope, and compassion** held here between the lines.

Who knows—your review might be the reason someone picks up this book and, in doing so, feels a little more understood, a tad less alone, and maybe even inspired to follow a quiet dream of their own.

Leave an honest rating or review in less than a minute

by scanning this with your camera app

SCAN ME

Your thoughts mean more than you know.

A GIFT FOR YOU

I've prepared something special to share with you:

Your Printable Set of 18 Self-Love Cards

Think of these as gentle whispers of self-care for your soul.

Perfect for your daily reflections, journaling,
or just as soft reminders of your majestic essence.

You'll also get an idea sheet with gentle ways to use your Soul Notes.

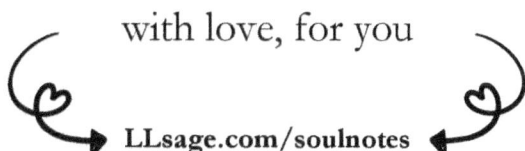

with love, for you

LLsage.com/soulnotes

If you choose to get the Soul Notes, you'll also get my studio letters,
with early access to new books, art, and words from the heart.

May these Soul Notes meet you where you are, with peace and joy.

Discover more from Leia Leh:
LLSAGE.com | @LLSAGE.art

www.ingramcontent.com/pod-product-compliance
Lightning Source LLC
LaVergne TN
LVHW041228080426
835508LV00011B/1113